WILD CATS

PREDATORS

Lynn M. Stone

Rourke Publications, Inc.
Vero Beach, Florida 32964

Edited by Sandra A. Robinson

PHOTO CREDITS
© Lynn M. Stone: cover, pages 4, 7, 10, 12, 13, 17,
18, 21; © Tom and Pat Leeson: title page, pages 8, 15

ACKNOWLEDGMENTS
The author thanks the Tallahassee Junior Museum
(Florida) for assistance in the preparation of some
photos for this book.

Library of Congress Cataloging-in-Publication Data

Stone, Lynn M.
   Wild cats / by Lynn Stone.
      p. cm. — (Predators)
   Includes index.
   Summary: Introduces bobcats, lynx, jaguars, and cougars, all
endangered wild cats of North America.
   ISBN 0-86625-441-2
   1. Felidae—North America—Juvenile literature. 2. Endangered
species—North America—Juvenile literature. [1. Felidae. 2. Rare
animals. 3. Predatory animals.] I. Title. II. Series: Stone, Lynn M.
Predators.
QL737.C23S785   1993
599.74'428'097—dc20   92-34499
                                       CIP
                                       AC

TABLE OF CONTENTS

WILD CATS AS PREDATORS

The wild cats are some of nature's deadliest **predators.** Predators hunt and kill other animals—their **prey**—to live.

The four best-known wild cats of North America are the jaguar, cougar, lynx and bobcat. For them, being able to catch another animal is the difference between living and dying.

In their soft fur coats, wild cats prowl about quietly and alertly on padded feet. They can also climb, leap and swim.

Wild cats prowl quietly on padded feet

WILD CAT WEAPONS

A wild cat's teeth are its main tools for killing. Its long front teeth are strong, sharp and slightly curved—perfect for stabbing its victim. Other teeth in a cat's mouth slice like knives.

The jaws of a cat are short, but they deliver a powerful bite. Jaguar jaws can crush a large animal's skull.

A cat's claws are sharp and curved to hold its prey. Unlike a dog's claws, cat claws are **retractable.** They can be withdrawn into a cat's paw like a turtle's head is pulled into its shell. Because they are extended only when holding prey, cat claws remain sharp.

The jaguar's bite is very powerful, even for a large cat

HOW WILD CATS HUNT

A hunting cat may hide and wait for prey in ambush, or it may **stalk** an animal. A stalking cat inches closer to its prey in quiet, careful steps. When the cat nears the prey, it leaps or charges.

A cat usually attacks from the rear or side of its prey. It kills by biting the prey's neck.

Cats hear extremely well, but they usually find prey by seeing it. Their eyes work well even in low light, so many cats are **nocturnal,** doing most of their hunting at night.

A Western cougar charges toward fleeing prey

BOBCATS

Bobcats look much like long-legged, overgrown tiger-striped house cats. However, bobcats weigh up to 35 pounds, which is much more than a house cat weighs.

Bobcats have short, "bobbed" tails, like lynxes, their close cousins.

Bobcats usually hunt birds, rabbits and rodents. They do much of their hunting at night.

Southern bobcats like forests and swamps. Bobcats in the West live in the desert and in mountain country. Throughout their range, from southern Canada into central Mexico, bobcats live in a variety of homes, or **habitats.**

A bobbed tail is the trademark of this bobcat and its Northern cousin, the lynx

The bobcat is at home in trees, as well as on the ground

The endangered ocelot is one of the smaller North American cats

LYNXES

The lynx is like a bobcat, but it has ear tufts—long, black hairs on the tips of its ears. Like the bobcat, the lynx is an excellent climber.

The lynx is at home in the cold evergreen forests of Canada. Big, furry paws help it travel easily on snow.

A lynx often hunts by ambushing smaller animals. Its favorite prey is the snowshoe rabbit, another creature whose feet are made for snow travel.

A bounding snowshoe rabbit dashes past a lynx

COUGARS

The cougar has several common names—mountain lion, puma and panther. It is a big, powerful cat with a long tail.

Despite its large size—up to 225 pounds—the cougar is graceful. It can leap 16 feet from the ground to an overhead tree limb or spring easily onto a deer.

Most North American cougars live from western Canada south into Mexico. Their habitat may be desert, swamp, mountain or forest.

The cougar lives in a wide variety of North American habitats, from Canada south into Mexico

JAGUARS

The jaguar is one of the world's truly *big* cats. A big male can weigh 250 pounds. The jaguar ranks in size only behind the tiger and lion.

Jaguars are heavier than their look-alike cousins, the leopards. Like leopards, which live in Africa and Asia, jaguars may be spotted or black.

Jaguars eat such creatures as armadillos, anteaters and deer. There is no animal living in jaguar country, except for large crocodiles, that the jaguar cannot kill.

No longer found in the southwestern United States, the jaguar lives in Mexico and south into Central and South America.

Jaguars may have spotted or black fur

WILD CATS AND PEOPLE

Wild cats generally fear people and avoid them. However, jaguars and cougars can be dangerous, especially to children.

Most people admire wild cats for their beauty, gracefulness and strength. Unfortunately, North America's wild cats have become vanishing animals in many places.

Cats have been hunted for sport and for their fur. They have also been killed by ranchers to protect their animals. The cats' greatest problem, however, has been the loss of living space.

The "Florida panther," the cougar of the Southeast, is nearly extinct

SAVING WILD CATS

Wildlife's living space—their habitat—disappears when people change wild lands into cities and farms. Largely because of lost habitat, many North American cats are **endangered**—in danger of disappearing, becoming **extinct.**

In Mexico and Central America the jaguar, ocelot, margay and some types of jaguarundi are endangered. (The ocelot and jaguarundi are also endangered in southern Texas.) Endangered, too, are the cougars of the Northeast and Florida.

Laws that protect wild cats help—but the future of North America's wild cats rests largely with the future of their habitats. These need our protection, too.

Glossary

endangered (en DANE jerd) — in danger of no longer existing; very rare

extinct (ex TINKT) — no longer existing

habitat (HAB uh tat) — the kind of place in which an animal lives, such as northern forest

nocturnal (nok TUR nul) — more active at night than in daytime

predator (PRED a tor) — an animal that kills another animal for food

prey (PRAY) — an animal or animals that are hunted for food by another animal

retractable (re TRAKT uh bul) — able to be withdrawn

stalk (STAWK) — hunting by moving slowly and quietly toward prey

INDEX